BETWEEN THE WHITE LINE AND THE FENCE POST

The true adventures of E.C. HERBERT'S two years of hitch-hiking around the United States 1968-1970

E.C. HERBERT

Cover Design by Outlaws Publishing LLC
Published by Outlaws Publishing LLC
July 2024
10 9 8 7 6 5 4 3 2 1

Dedicated to Gabe & Dave

PROLOGUE

My earliest memories of traveling occurred when I was four or five years old, although I had been traveling since I was born, just too young to remember it. You see, my dad was a lumberjack and also a crop picker. Our summer months were spent in New Hampshire, where dad worked in the woods as a lumberjack cutting down trees or running a sawmill.

The winter months were spent in Florida, where he picked crops.

Sitting here typing, I can close my eyes and still hear the high pitched humming of the mill's huge circular saw blade as it cuts through a log, turning it into a flat piece of wood which is called a board.

Just before school started up in the fall, Ma and Dad would pack up whatever type of vehicle we owned at that time and set off for the warmer climate of Florida and the citrus groves where dad would work as a crop picker. We would make our home there along with other migrant workers through the winter months. This went on until I was about ten years old when dad was helping a friend roof his house, just before we were to leave for Florida. Well, Dad got careless and fell off the roof, breaking his right leg and also his back. Dad would have his leg amputated and spend the next two years in a body cast. He never fully recovered and was unable to do any traveling. As a result, I grew up in Laconia, New Hampshire where we had family. I used to kid the old man by asking him why he hadn't fallen out of an orange tree in Florida where it was warm.

I was born in February, 1950 in a small town in Florida called Polk City. Polk City was a citrus growing community located halfway between Orlando and Lakeland on Highway Four. My mom always referred to me as her Florida Cracker 'cause I was born in that state.

Traveling, I remember my bed for these trips was the floorboard area in the back where mom had made up a cocoon like area out of blankets. Between the humming of the tires and the warmth of the air coming from under the front seat and into my little cocoon, I would be asleep almost instantly.

As I write this now, I can close my eyes and once again hear the humming of those tires and feel the warmth coming into my little cocoon home from under the front seat. I have often wondered if this was the reason behind me lacking nighttime driving skills.

Just the humming of the tires would bring back memories of those times, so many years ago, that my eyelids would flutter and I could feel sleep coming on.

This is just a glimpse back in time to set my history for love of travel and the unknown which lurked around every corner and with every new person who would stop and graciously extend a ride to complete strangers.

My real adventures that this book is about wouldn't take place until after I graduated from high school in the summer of 1968.

No other time in history was a decade defined as clearly as the sixties were. The 60's gave birth to such bands as: The Beatles, the Grateful Dead, Rolling Stones, Cream, Jimi Hendrix Experience, and on and on and on, way too many to list.

You had 1960-66 defined as the Early Hippie stage. 1967 as the Summer-of-Love, and 1967-69 as the Revolution. Yup! California was the place to be at this time, especially, San Francisco's Haight Ashbury region which gave birth to the Hippie Culture and FREE LOVE, PEACE, SEX, DRUGS and ROCK & ROLL.

Between the White Line and the Fence Post refers to that strip of ground that borders the blacktop and the landscape, better known as the breakdown lane, or shoulder.

Most highways had guide rails or fences five or six feet back from there to deflect any vehicles which happen to go off the road.

In most states back then, and true even today, you couldn't hitch hike on the interstates. Because of that law, many a night was spent in the local lockup. Most of the time if we were caught, we would be driven to the outskirts of jurisdiction of the Highway Patrol Officer who didn't want to do all the paperwork that was involved for such a penny-ante offense. Those rides always came with the warning to be careful and to, STAY INSIDE THE WHITE LINE.

Note: If anyone reading this book has had this same experience, go onto my website and leave me a message. www.echerbert.com

In case you wonder about my memory to recall routes, I used a map to help refresh some of the places and events.

I hope you enjoy reading about some of the events that shaped a decade and would be recorded in history books.

Early History

Graduating from high school that hot summer day in June brought on a whole boat load of mixed emotions.

First, I was the only one in the whole Herbert line to graduate high school, a promise I had made my mom years ago. Even if there wasn't this promise, I still would have graduated to fulfill a promise that I had made myself.

The military career I thought I would have, I learned three weeks earlier would never happen.

The Viet Nam conflict was still raging and I wanted to join my friends. Because both my mom and dad were unable to work, I had supported them through the part time jobs I did while still in school. In the eyes of the Army, this classified me as the sole supporting son.

Being their only son added to it. I was classified as the only son, so the military didn't want me. I would find out years later that mom and dad had been in contact with the Army recruiting officer in Laconia and that is how the whole supporting issue came into play and why I was rejected.

I was devastated and it would be years before I would forgive either one of them. So I stayed home and watched, while my best friends signed up and left for boot camp.

Some would return, many wouldn't.

My days of mourning were short lived as the roar of the first Harley motorcycles filled the air signaling the beginning of what is known as bike weekend or motorcycle weekend. I will write more later-on concerning bike weekend.

Of the many motorcycle weekends I had survived in previous years, this one would be different and forever change my life. In some ways, it molded me into the person I am today. If you didn't live in the sixties, you missed one of the greatest time periods of the century.

It is difficult to put into words that which defines this space in time. So much was happening.

Never was there a time in history that was defined by such a vast array in happenings. The United States would undergo an invasion from abroad. No, not the kind of invasion that involves guns and military, but one that involves drums, guitars and a vast amount of drugs and psychedelic music. The Beatles, Doors, Rolling Stones, the Byrd's, Hendrix, Joplin, and the list goes on and on.

Drugs, such as 'acid' aka LSD (psychedelic's) smack, speed, uppers & downers, and pot, all gave rise in the sixties. And let's not forget those little foul tasting things known as Psilocybin mushrooms. Better known as *"shrooms"* or *"magic mushrooms."*

This was a time where you could visit any place you wanted and never leave your house.

Phrases such as *Flower Power, Groovy, Far Out, Make Love Not War, Peace,* were only a few from that era.

Tie dye clothes became very popular during this time period thanks to a rock star known as Janis Joplin.

I became very efficient in tie dying and sold tee shirts I had made down on the board walk at the Weirs Beach. To this day, the brightly colored tie dyed clothes can be found in most department stores and gift shops, no matter where you go.

Bell bottoms, love beads, and granny glasses surfaced during this time period also.

And let's not forget the vast array of smoking paraphernalia.

Bell bottomed pants had been around since the early 1800's being part of a sailor's uniform.

The 60's would give bell bottoms a new birth by introducing them into main stream public and would remain until the early 80's, and not re-surface till the early 1990's where they would also undergo a name change. Now known as *"boot-cut"* and would be a major fashion design. This comeback was short lived and would give way to *"skinny-jeans"*

I'm only putting this in so you, the reader, can see that this time period had some major impact on the years ahead, even in the world of fashion.

The Viet Nam conflict would divide families, cause riots and put a sour taste in many mouths as parents watched their sons march off to war.

For the 1st time in history, the news media was allowed to film on location, live! This brought the fighting and death into every American home.

The sixties would also see the assassination of President John Kennedy, Martian Luther King Jr, Bobby Kennedy, Malcom X. and Medgar Evers.

We even landed a *MAN ON THE MOON* in the sixties!

Ya, it would be hard to define the sixties using any other word than "Awesome." And here I was, just coming to age right in the middle of it all and wanting to get my butt out to San Francisco and join the movement out there.

My half-brother Bob had left Connecticut in 1963 and moved to Sausalito, Ca. which was an artist colony just over the Golden Gate Bridge from San Francisco, and also saw the invasion of the so called *Hippies.* Sausalito would become my part-time home as Dave and I would leave and travel to whatever place was making the headlines.

In the summer of 1966, Bob drove out to visit, so we planned on me driving back with him when he decided to leave. Mom and dad weren't too keen on that idea, but I promised to be back in time to start school. Secretly, I didn't plan on returning to New Hampshire, but moving in and working for Bob. He had started a painting business when he first arrived in Sausalito, and in a short period of time he became well known and was booked into the following year.

I had worked for my Uncle in Connecticut the previous two summers learning how to paint houses. "Unc" as I called him, had a painting business and I wanted to learn so I could start my own business.

My plans were to finish high school, go into the service, do my time, then once out, move to California and paint with Bob or maybe even start up my own business in New Hampshire, which was looking more promising than working for my brother.

As we drove cross-country, I learned a lot of what my brother was like and what to expect living and working for him. I had made up my mind, even before we arrived in California, that I would be coming home and fall back on plan B which was to finish school, to go into the military and serve my time. Once out, to start-up my own painting business.

Everything was going as planned right up to the point when I wasn't accepted into the military.

The first day out of school found me and my good friend Jimmy on the roof of a local homeowner with paint brushes in our hands. I had found this job through one of the Ames boys whose dad owned several of the arcades in the Weirs and who my dad also worked for mowing lawns around all of his hotels.

Once I started painting, several passers-by's stopped and ask me about painting their places. The best thing here was I didn't need to travel to any other job, as the houses were right here at the Weirs.

My friend Jim turned out to be a good painter, so it wasn't long before this job was done and we moved onto the next. I had gotten over not being able to join the military and now had sights set on getting enough cash together for my move out west to California.

The Weirs was also a mecca of long haired, pot smoking, *Hippies,* and you could have guessed, I was right in the middle of it all.

I had spoken to Jimmy and told him my plans for California.

Jimmy was deciding whether to come with me or not as he had met a girl and was at once smitten by her.

"Bike Week" of 1965 which had turned into a riot as two "outlaw" motorcycle clubs decided to challenge each other.

What it turned into was several other clubs joining in and before you knew it, cars were flipped over and set on fire. The local police and National Guard were called in to calm things down, which they did but not before there was lots of damage done to local businesses.

And you guessed it! l was in the middle of it all!!! And I have my share of scars to prove it.

Two things would come about because of this.

One being, that the once known Motorcycle Week would be reduced to just a week-end, making it now known as Motorcycle Week-end. It would stay a three-day event until the early 90's. Businesses wanting to draw more business decided to once again make Motorcycle Week-end a seven-day affair and Motorcycle Week was once again and still is to this day.

Second. One year when Motorcycle Week was ending, I found a long haired stranger on my doorstep one morning. We will call him Dave. Dave was in bad shape. He told me that the night before, he was jumped by several motorcycle gang members who beat him to a pulp and stole his motorcycle.

I, being only fifteen, didn't really know what to think so I helped him up and brought him inside. My mom instantly started to size up the issue at hand. Before you knew it, she had a bucket of hot water and some towels and started to clean him up. Dad wanted to throw him out but mom told him no.

A short time later, Dave appeared from under the dirt and dried blood that had covered his face. Mom had found no real big cuts that need stitches but several small ones and what appeared to be a broken nose and a couple holes in his jaw where teeth used to be.

Dave wore the same size shirts as I did but my pants were long on him, and besides, they were *bell-bottoms!* This didn't matter as mom brought out the sewing machine and hemmed a couple pair of my jeans for him along with straightening the legs.

Dave and I quickly bonded as brothers and little did we know what was in store for our friendship in the coming years.

That summer we grew closer, doing everything together. Drugs had entered the picture. Dave liked pot, where I was smitten with LSD.

There were a few times Dave would disappear and mom and I would worry until he returned. The only thing we would get from him was that he had gone home for a few days.

He told us that he was from a town north of Laconia but gave little other information about his life. Later on our paths would go in different directions as we both fought to gain our own identity.

Our paths would cross only one time once we returned to New Hampshire, and then we would never see one another again. I have learned of his passing and the rough times he had fighting the many devils that lived inside. Never overcoming them, but feeding them till they devoured him.

That summer, Dave and I started hitch-hiking all over the place. We enjoyed going to different places and meeting different people both young and old.

We spent time in Boston's Harvard Square and New York's Central Park. Even after I got a driver's license and a car, we would continue to hitch-hike.

Well, that summer ended and I went back to school and Dave went wherever Dave went. We would not have any contact at all until the next year's "Motorcycle Week-end" at which time we seemed to pick up right where we had left off. I had started letting my hair grow and started a beard also. We weren't allowed long hair and facial hair in school so it would only be for the summer.

Drugs flowed around everywhere that summer. I tried them all and decided that they were not for me except LSD, but had to experience them anyways (that would change rather quickly). Now Dave, that was a different story.

Dave liked pot.

Although at this time I didn't smoke pot, or do drugs, I discovered that a lot of money could be made in selling them and the one that was the easiest to buy and re-sell was LSD. LSD could be purchased in many forms. I chose what was known as "Micro-dots" This was a small tablet, the size of a saccharine artificial sugar pill which I could purchase in Boston or New York for ten cents a "hit" and sell them three hits for five dollars.

It wasn't long before I earned the nick-name of "acid man." If you wanted some LSD, you bought from me. Soon my "purple haze" painted VW *Hippie* bus gave way to a bright red 1956 Chevy Convertible. The state wouldn't let me put Acid-Man on the plate so I put my second nick-name "NOSE". Many who don't remember me by name remembers that '56 red Convertible with that license plate (someone on Facebook contacted me and remembered pulling up next to me and smiling to himself. His license plate bore the word *Ears*).

I know some of you are bored by now wanting me to get on with the story but I wanted you all to feel this time in history. The 60's sure would go down as a time in our history.

Chapter 1

"Damn, that water's cold!!!"

It was a hot, humid late June morning of 1968 when Dave and I packed our backpacks and accepted our first ride of our adventure. That first ride coming from my mom who drove us to Concord, New Hampshire and dropped us off with words of encouragement and a prayer for safe travels.

Dave and I wanted to say we hitched from coast to coast so we headed to the shores of New Hampshire where we would shed our shoes and walk into the Atlantic Ocean and end with the same in the Pacific Ocean.

For all of you familiar with the Atlantic Ocean and the New Hampshire coastline, you know exactly what I mean when I use the expression, "Damn, that water's cold."

Even when I have swum in the Atlantic in Florida, I still use that expression when voicing the water temperature.

From Concord to the coast, route 4 to Portsmouth would be the quickest, most direct route to take even though it wasn't a major turnpike.

Well! There was nothing quick about route 4 and we learned quickly that if you wanted to get from point A to point B, the fastest would be turnpike or highway, not a backward, single lane road.

We were aware of that, but how quickly we forget in moments of excitement. Also, good to have several black magic markers and a road map. Just knowing where you wanted to go wasn't good enough. You also needed to know how to get there.

Having officially stepped into the Atlantic, it was now time to really start our trip.

As far as it goes there was only one way to California. Route 66. "The Mother Road"

I can look on it now and smile and shake my head as I see that sign we had made in advance that read, GHICAGO RT 66…funny now!

Getting from Portsmouth, New Hampshire to the heart of Chicago, Illinois. And the start of Route 66 was no easy task and one we abandoned rather quickly. In place, Boston, Massachusetts seemed good, because we had hitched to Boston on a number of occasions in the past.

Turning our Chicago sign over and with marker wrote Boston in the largest letters we could. Within ten minutes, we had a ride that would take us all the way to Boston.

Although we had hitched a lot, we had never used signs. Lesson learned was to always write in the name of the next largest city you wanted to go to.

It was also at this time our plans changed. As badly as we wanted to hitch from one end of Route 66 to the other, we decided that could wait until later. We would hitch around the east coast and see some of the sights and, as rides directed, let them plot our course.

It would be almost three months before we found ourselves in Springfield, Missouri and truly our start over Route 66.

That first ride to Boston was one I hardly remember now.

The driver, being a long-hair, was going down to see a girl he had just met not two weeks before. His name and his girlfriend's name escapes me now, but I met another guy I'll call Dan who I purchased some pot and LSD from and who later would become my largest supplier of LSD, as this would become my favorite and my most money maker.

Dave and I spent maybe three days crashing with Dan. In that time, I met some very shady characters.

Most of my days were spent down at the Commons just hanging and grooving with the large number of *Hippies* that seemed to have migrated there.

Although there was much gaiety in the air, along with the constant smell of Pot, there was also much anguish to be seen. For every one *Flower Child* happily skipping around bestowing love and kisses on everyone, there was someone yelling and screaming and clawing at themselves in an attempt to rid their bodies of some *dark demon* who had invaded their drug induced minds.

Harvard Square, a miniature Boston Common, was basically the same except the crowds were a few years younger being that Harvard University was close by and probably more *re-fined Hippies.*

The streets around the square were lined with shops that sold everything from *bong pipes* to all kinds of *Hippie Culture paraphernalia.*

A couple of years later, I would return to one of these shops and purchase my first piece of jewelry for a very special girl I had met.

There was an endless supply of drugs and girls that came and went and fun was had by all. Dave disappeared for a day and when he returned, we decided it was time to move on.

Dan gave us a ride to the on-ramp of the interstate.

Thanking him and watching him pull away from the entrance ramp was almost a sad occasion. The three days spent there seemed, in some ways like three months and in others like three minutes.

Either way, Dave and I were now ready to continue on.

The first few cars to pass by tooted their horns and waved.

A pick-up truck pulled over, just past us, and tooted his horn. Dave and I picked up our packs and hurried towards him, only to have him squeal away, giving us the finger as he did.

We were now in front of the sign that warned against hitch-hiking and bikes on the highway. So here we stood waiting for our next ride, holding up our simple signs that read, "NY CITY."

Chapter 2

"The Village & Time Square, New York"

Greenwich Village was the most popular spot to be in during the 60's & 70's. It was more of a birthplace for artist and music icons such as Bob Dylan, Jimi Hendrix and some of the early folk music groups as to the Hippie Culture but had to go there just because.

I hadn't seen so many people in one place as the Village, outside of Bike Week.

Dave and I spent some time visiting the many coffee shops, hoping to run into Dylan but never did. And it wasn't long before we started to feel the stares of the people there. Maybe it was the way we were dressed or our back-packs, but we were out of place. Today I can say with surety it was our appearance, knowing that even back then, real-estate was the highest in the country so everyone there were well to do and here we were completely out of their league and they didn't mind letting us know that.

Dave and I would find out during our travels that *not everyone embraced the Hippie Movement.*

Even today in 2016, The Village is still a popular tourist attraction and artist community. It is the center point for the LGBT community. Today, at least in my point of view, The Village is the east coast's San Francisco.

Nothing real exciting to write about concerning The Village but, Time Square is a different story!

The Center of the Universe. This is just one name that Time Square has been labeled with and for all of you out there, if you weren't old enough to have been there during the 60's-70's then I can tell you honestly, and first hand, pictures don't do Time Square justice.

Gone today are the live Peep shows, XXX movie theaters, drunks, bums, prostitutes, the god-awful-smell of Lysol everywhere which was a mainstay of the *Red Light District*, also known as Time Square.

The first thing we did was to find a locker storage where we could unload our back packs. We were excited to see everything and didn't want to worry about our stuff being stolen or getting mugged because of them.

It amazes me just what our minds can store and remember.

I could vividly describe everything that I witnessed and took part in at this time of our journey, but would have to give this book a different rating and keep it out of the hands of my grandkids.

During the "60's" the country was a different place to live in, and live it we did.

Chapter 3

"Kent State University, Ohio"

One thing about being on the road was how flexible you become in a short period of time. When we started out, we would map a course where we wanted to go, but after a time, events of the day that were happening in the country directed our travel.

We were someplace in the mid-west, when the shootings of four college students took place at Kent State University in Kent, Ohio. And you guessed it, out came our pieces of cardboard and markers and a new sign was made for Kent, Ohio.

I was a little leery, at first, listening to the news on the car radios from those who picked us up, but Dave always wanted to be in the center-of-the-storm, so to speak.

Sometimes this proved to be a good thing others not so good. Kent State was not a good thing. The shootings, which left four students dead, was done by the Ohio Army National Guard as the students gathered to protest the invasion of Cambodia during the Vietnam War. By the time we reached Kent, Ohio, it was probably four days after the shootings. The University was closed and now Dave and I occupied a jail cell.

Pot and other drugs were easy to get, so we never traveled with any kinds of drugs on us, always aware that we could be stopped by local cops or Highway Patrol or State Troopers at any time. Good thing!

Tension was still high in Kent, so when the first police cruiser passed by, it went really slow trying to observe us. Within three or four minutes, the same cruiser returned followed by two others. As they approached, they sped up, fanned out and surrounded us. Seconds later, five drawn guns were pointed at us and several of the cops were screaming, "On the ground!! On the ground!!!"

We were then picked up, thrown against a cruiser, and frisked. Our back packs were torn open and its contents dumped out onto the street. By now, several other vehicles had passed, many blowing their horns and yelling profanities at the police, which surely didn't help our situation any.

We were brought to the station, fingerprinted and put in a cell to wait as our identities were checked. In this cell were three other men who kept giving us the once over and were saying nasty things concerning Hippies and long haired people.

Dave finally had enough and made a jester with his raised finger which caused all hell to break out inside the cell before the police could get in to us. To this day, I think the police knew exactly what was going to happen to us.

Thank god we only suffered cuts and bruises and no broken bones or worse. I remember we were taken and put in a different cell where we stayed for several more hours before being released and taken outside with a warning not to show our faces there again and another warning against hiking on the Interstate.

Walking through an alley, we found a dumpster and a cardboard box which we tore the flaps off, then walked to the entrance ramp of the highway, took out our black marker and made the next sign.

Chapter 4

"Washing windows, Pumping gas"

It was about six months into our journey where Dave and I had become professionals at two things: *Window washing and Pumping gas.*

When money would run out or get low, we would spend a couple of days in a town looking for odd jobs we could do to raise a few bucks for food and a couple of joints, or whatever we could find.

I had worked at Franks Texaco in Laconia, so that's what we did. We would stop at a gas station and ask for some odd jobs to perform. Once the owner heard our story, he would hire us to pump gas and to wash the station's windows, but most of time was spent sitting with the owner and several of his buddies who he would call and they would come down, sometimes with cold beers, and just sit and listen as we told some of our stories of life on the road.

It was funny how many cars would pass the station honking their horns and yelling Peace. Once our presence was known, patrons would swing in and hand us sandwiches and soft drinks. We sometimes would meet some other kids like ourselves who we would party with after the station closed.

A long-haired Hippie, pumping gas in some small hick town would also draw lots of attention, especially with the girls, moms, and even grandma's. I pumped a lot of gas where I was told, "Can I have a dollar's worth, please." Just enough to get their windshield washed. This followed with a sexy smile, spread legs, mini skirt, and no panties. More girls and women went both braless and no panties during the "60's" and here I was, washing car windows and enjoying the sights.

In those times when we decided to stay in a town for a couple of days, Dave would sometimes disappear until the agreed time we were going to leave and out of nowhere it seemed Dave would show back up and we would once again be on the road.

At one station I pumped gas, the owner had a friend who owned a factory that he wanted us to wash all the windows. We agreed, sight unseen. What a mistake! Three story high building with probably five hundred windows.

No scuffling, just ladders we sat up and straddled them with 2x8 planking. We did have enough sense to tie us off, just in case we were to have a fall.

You wouldn't believe how many offers we had to wash personal home windows.

When we were in a town pumping gas or washing windows, we never lacked for anything, food, drink, drugs, or a bed which usually came occupied.

If you could name it, or think it, well, we did it!

Today when I pump my own gas, at least one memory passes through my brain reminding me of the hundreds of gas tanks I filled, and the hundreds of bare chested, no panties women I saw while washing their windshields.

To this day, I refuse to wash windows.

Chapter 5

"Rednecks and Pickups"

Route 66 through the Texas Panhandle up until we reached Amarillo was boring and long. At least, it seemed so.

There wasn't much to see and it was hot and dry.

Texas in the sixties wasn't the most friendly state if you had long hair, wore bell bottoms and looked the part of the Hippie culture. Dave and I fit that bill.

Cars would pull past us only to speed away after running to reach them. It wasn't uncommon to have beer bottles and cans tossed at us from passing cars and trucks.

It felt like we walked damn near the whole length of the Panhandle.

Once we saw a train in the distance across this wide prairie, we decided we would run at an angle to it and hop on it. It was going west and so were we.

At the distance it was away it looked like it would be easy.

Dave and I had been talking about hopping a train and here was our chance. Not!!! That train must have been traveling thirty miles an hour, if not more. No way to hop that one, so we walked and walked.

We saw "beep, beep" the Road Runner and "Wile E. Coyote" in the panhandle.

That first night, we slept out under a sky alive with the twinkling of a bazillion stars. It was peaceful and quiet, but still hot, hot, hot.

Next morning, armed with our cardboard signs that said "Amarillo," found us once again between the white line and the fence post having been warned several times by Highway Police against hitching on the highway.

To this day, I do believe that Texas was ten years behind the rest of the country. I don't think the Hippie Movement ever entered Texas space, except for the city of Austin which was where we were headed with our drug induced brains and the fact we were on our beloved Route 66, once again. We decided to go to Amarillo, once there, backtrack and head south to Austin and the McGregor County Park which held a large Hippie Community. From there, continue to San Antonio and go see The Alamo, but first we needed to get to Amarillo.

In the Texas heat, Dave and I were soon shirtless and sitting on our backpacks smoking a joint when a red pickup went by. As it approached, we stood up and held up our signs pointing to them vigorously and holding up our lit joint as an offering for a lift.

What we got were unfriendly hand jesters and unfriendly stares by the three cowboys in the cab. The truck sped away and Dave and I returned to our seats on the backpacks.

It was hot and we were pretty stoned when the same red pickup returned. It went by then turned around and pulled up beside us and offered us a lift. Leery, we tossed our packs in the back and hopped aboard. Once seated, the truck sped off.

I motioned to Dave and showed him I had already taken my switchblade from my sneaker and cradled it in my palm. I hunched my shoulders a signal of "just in case."

Suddenly, the driver pulled the truck off the road onto a dirt path that went out across the plains, stopping when it arrived where several other pickups were stopped. This was not the time for knives, so we quickly returned them to where we had them hid. Soon, a group of about ten kids all about our age wearing cowboy hats surrounded the truck we were in.

Dave reached into his backpack and pulled out a baggie of pot and offered it to them.

As one reached up for it, Dave suddenly punched him in the mouth and jumped down and just started wailing on whoever was the closest.

For a minute, his outburst caught them by surprise, then, things got serious. I was pulled from the truck and beat into unconsciousness. I might have got a couple hits in, I don't recall.

How long I was out I couldn't say, except it was late in the day when I came around.

Minutes passed before I gained my senses and realized I was buck naked and tied to a fence post. Looking around for Dave, I saw him in the same condition I was in, except he was still out. His body was a bloody mess and for a moment, I thought he was dead. His hair had been cut off along with his beard and was in a pile at his feet. I realized then, I was in the same condition. Hairless!

Hairless! Yes, but still alive. I tried calling out to him and found out that I had a few less teeth in the front of my mouth. Finally, on his own, I saw Dave start to move then open his eyes through the caked on blood.

"Well! Ain't this bull shit." He said through his clinched mouth, then started to laugh which brought him much pain. I started to laugh also, the best I could. Today, I know that laughter was one of celebration to be alive. The way we were hog tied to the post with duct tape, I knew we weren't getting loose. I don't think there was an inch of my body that didn't feel pain of some sort. Looking around I saw where they had scattered the contents of our back packs on the ground but not before cutting them to shreds.

Once the sun went down, it got dark pretty quickly. I was scared knowing we were both at the mercy of any animal which came by looking for a meal. Tied there helpless and having been so near death, so many thoughts invade your mind along with so many promises if ever you were to be set free again, and how quickly you forget them later on. In the darkness you could see the far off headlights of passing cars, but knowing they couldn't see you. Along with the Texas night, came the nights drop in temperature. Soon, both of us could be heard shivering. Although cold, I knew it wasn't cold enough to freeze us to death.

A set of headlights turning off the highway caught my attention. The one was followed by several others. Looks like they are returning to finish the job. I said to Dave, through clenched, shivering, mouth.

As the vehicles got close, it was plain to see that the front one was indeed a red pickup truck. But, unlike earlier, it was driven by an adult male who stopped right next to me and flung open the driver's door and jumped out amongst the cloud of dust he had produced. The other vehicles came to a stop and several men jumped out. Dave and I were soon wrapped in blankets speeding to the nearest hospital. I was told that one of the boys from earlier had told his dad about what had happened and the dad in return contacted some of the other dads and came to our rescue. Dave and I were well taken care of. We both had some cracked ribs which hurt like hell for several weeks after, but nothing permanent.

Once out of the hospital, we spent several days with the family of the boy who told his dad about us. In that time, two mothers took us shopping for new clothes and new back packs. We got our heads shaved and they even brought us shopping for wigs. I would have my hair back, longer than before. It would take some time to grow back the beard. A dentist visit for us both and our smiles were once again teeth-filled. Even once my hair grew back, I kept that wig, as a reminder of what was, but also what could have been.

Well, new clothes, hair, teeth and five hundred dollars each and a ride to the highway will sum up this portion of the trip through Texas.

Chapter 6

"The Commune"

In Dave's and my book, you couldn't take on the real title of "Hippie" until you experienced living in a Commune, but how do you find a Commune? You might be thinking that why not make up a cardboard sign and instead of having a city on it, simply have Commune. Right? Well, it was almost that easy.

Outside of a couple bad experiences, most of our rides were from other "long hairs" and believe me, two years on the road, you met a lot of them. Unlike what most adults thought, they were the smart ones.

Anyway, want to know what's going on in a town or city? Ask a "long hair." That's how we found our Commune. Commune's come in all sizes and colors and came into being for many different reasons. Kids looking to get away from parental authority, troubled teens, runaways…etc. The list goes on and on. I was hoping to find one where everyone chipped in and did chores such as gardening and such, living off the land, listening to Ravi Shankar and taking LSD trips.

The commune Dave and I was introduced into was more or less a weekend, "get away from the parents" commune. Our commune was in a gravel pit, made up of makeshift living quarters in VW buses and the bed of pickup trucks plus a few tents. The gravel pit was one that had been abandoned years ago. There was a large swimming hole that was a pit, which had filled up will water. Our ride who took us out there was one of these weekend Hippies. It was like a commune because everyone shared whatever they had. Beer, pot, LSD and in the case of some of the girls, their bodies! We learned that the local police knew all about what went on there and chose not to interfere as long as they created no trouble and the police didn't get any complaints from any parents. By Friday afternoon, there must have been twenty-five or thirty people there, both guys and girls.

Dave and I soon became the center of attention as we stood and walked around a large campfire relating stories of our journey and the places we had been and the people we had met. There were no, what we considered "hard drugs" there. As mentioned, beer, pot, and LSD.

The weekend was spent skinny dipping in the water hole, being in a drug induced or alcohol induced stupor, storytelling, and romping with the many girls who showed up. When not storytelling, music blared from an eight-track tape someone had attached some portable speakers to.

On one of our rides, I heard a song on the radio from a new band called Grand Funk Railroad and asked if anyone had heard of them. Someone had and next day I was driven into town where I found an eight track tape and bought it. "On Time" was their first release and although it sold millions it would be their release of

"Closer to Home" in 1970 which they became noted for. My favorite band at that time. Needless to say, no one listened to Ravi Shankar!

Chapter 7

"Golden Gate Park aka Needle Park"

Finally made it to California and "WOW" one hundred fourteen degrees in the shade. This high temperature was normal, this time of the year. After all, this was Needles, California, located in the Mojave Desert region. Two days earlier, it had been one hundred nineteen degrees.

We had taken a ride from a man with a white Cadillac convertible towing a U-Haul trailer just outside of Albuquerque, New Mexico going to Needles to deliver a piece of equipment. He had a deadline and was hoping to pick up someone who could help him drive.

We were on our beloved Route 66 again. There were several places we wanted to stop and spend some time, but we decided to forgo stopping for the direct ride to California.

This ride would also be my and Dave's first time doing what was known as Reds and Yellow Jackets. Both well-known pills in the trucking trade as ones to keep you awake for long periods of time. Dave took a liking to them, where I didn't. I have always loved my sleep, and when I want to sleep, I want to sleep.

The exit for the Grand Canyon was hard to pass up, but California was just ahead and that Caddie's speedometer was set on ninety-five anyways. "To hitch a ride out of Needles! Are you kidding me?" Nothing moves in that heat except the Trailways bus. So, onto the bus station. I was surprised a ticket to San Francisco was so cheap. I know now it was because it took three full days, and god knows how many bus changes to get there. We could have bought more expensive, direct tickets there but didn't know that, seeing this was our first travel by bus experience. Later on in my career, I would drive this exact route many times and get a chance to stop at the many places I would have liked to back then, but being on a bus, I couldn't. There was this little black girl who was a runaway that Dave got to know during the bus trip. I hadn't realized two people could get in so many different positions on a bus seat!!!

Arriving in Sacramento, I would call my brother who lived in Sausalito to come and pick us up, which he did. He was surprised to see us. We both stayed with him and visited Sausalito Square which was in the heart of Sausalito and a Hippie hangout. Sausalito was an artist colony and attracted all kinds of people, Hippies and Love Children were part of the Sausalito makeup. Two days after arriving in Sausalito found us walking across the Golden Gate Bridge. If anyone has driven across the bridge but never has walked it, next time you have the opportunity, park and walk across it. Unbelievable!

Walking into Golden Gate Park, Dave and I were confronted almost immediately by a couple of addicts looking to score, as we had entered that part of the park which had been titled "Needle Park." It was the home of those homeless addicts where everyone shared a needle which later lead to major AIDS spread for that reason alone.

My brother had told us all about this section of the park and had warned us against being there and to find the section which was named "Hippie Hill." Now, here were our kind. Free spirited, long haired, colorfully dressed, pot smoking, LSD droppers. "Our kind of people."

Janis Joplin, Jefferson Airplane, the Grateful Dead were known to come here and play for free, but never while we were there. We did however, locate the famous Carousal and rode it. Later on, before we decided to head for home, we returned to my brother's place and I painted with him for a couple of weeks to earn some traveling money.

Dave would disappear for a couple of days, then return to my brother's place, all messed up. I think it was at this time, Dave picked up the monkey that followed him the rest of his life.

Soon, time to hit the road again. We had seen California and had been to those places we had heard about. I will include "Haight Ashbury" simply because I'm sure many have heard about it and its role in the "Hippie Movement." The highlight of Haight Ashbury was the "Summer of Love" which was in 1967. WE wouldn't be there till much later when it was a rundown drug infested area that the police even refused to enter. So, if you want to experience "Haight Ashbury at this time you will have to do a Google search on it. I wish we would have been there at that time as it was the center of the "Hippie Culture."

My brother was going to drive us to Sacramento but decided to drive us all the way to Reno, Nevada instead.

Reno, Nevada, another, not so fun place to be!

Chapter 8

"Girls Galore"

Reno turned out to be a very unfriendly place, if you were a long hair. The place we wanted to be was Sparks, Nevada, just to the north of Reno. You would think that a state with no speed laws would be interested in hitch hikers but that was not the case.

All through Nevada we were harassed. You couldn't be on any interstate highway. You had to hitch from the entrance before the sign that said no hitch hiking, bikes, etc.

Having spent a few days in Sparks with a bunch of guys who had picked us up, we were ready to leave. Very little traffic headed east from Sparks. After several hours, we decided to do something we hadn't done before. We decided to separate with plans to meet somewhere along the route later.

I went into the woods while Dave held out his sign. What a surprise when the first car stopped and picked him up. Once they were gone, I felt sort of scared and vowed that if we did meet up again, we would not separate again.

I wasn't so lucky. About two hours passed before a car stopped and picked me up. The driver was probably around sixty or so. Sitting next to him was a woman looking to be about the same age. Both were well dressed having just come from the casino's in Reno. They asked who I was and where I was going. Typical of this whole trip.

Falling asleep I was later shaken awake asking if that was my friend. Trying to focus my eyes on the side of the road, I indeed see Dave hitching. They pulled over and stopped. Dave sure was surprised to see me in the back seat. We wouldn't separate again.

Soon, a joint was lit in the front seat and handed back to us. That started it. Then, the old lady had climbed over the seat and she was now in Dave's lap. She grabbed my hands to place them on her body but I wasn't interested. I must have fallen asleep, because when I woke, the car had stopped and I found myself alone. Looking out the window we were parked in a driveway of a very large ranch home. I recollect waking up and it was light. Now looking out the window I saw the smiling faces of several girls looking in at me. Story being, this old couple ran a home for teenage runaway girls.

We spent about three weeks there helping with needed repairs. Paint, some carpenter work, widows replaced, and some fences repaired. The girls as well as the old woman would walk around more often than not in bra and panties, hug and kiss and do whatever to entice us.

There wasn't a minute in the day that went by where Dave and I weren't enticed in one way or another. It was like living in a triple X movie and when it became too much to fight off, it was time to leave. But not before!

We decided to head south and to the Grand Canyon and back on route 66.

29

Chapter 9

"End of an Era"

Even out in the north mid-west the Woodstock Music Festival was heard of. A call home confirmed it. So in August, we set our sights on returning east to partake in what would go down in history as the largest event of a generation of music and Hippies, while a war was going on. A peaceful anti-war demonstration.

As we traveled, we were in contact with several friends and had everything lined up so when we got home everyone was waiting for us. It was exciting and something new to talk about with the many different rides we got. Everyone was in awe at the two Hippies hitching from state to state.

As we got nearer to our home, several rides we had were from Hippies headed to upper state New York to attend the festival. We could have forgone going to New Hampshire and just went with one of the rides. But I had made plans, so to New Hampshire I went where Dave stayed on with one of the rides with plans of finding each other there. Right!

No one predicted what an event Woodstock would turn into, even knowing some of the bands planning on playing there. Others would seemingly come out of the woodwork. Woodstock was billed as "Three days of Peace & Music" in opposition to the Vietnam War.

A short visit when I reach home with the folks, then it was off to New York and Woodstock! Here, I would love to have some great stories concerning Woodstock to write about, but I don't. Three quarters of the way there, it started to rain and they were predicting it all weekend. So, I had my friends pull over and drop me off. They would continue on to the greatest event of our time and I would return home, tired and happy not to think about spending time in the rain, knowing the bands wouldn't play in the rain anyways. There are some great reads and pictures of Woodstock, if interested in learning more.

Dave would return to New Hampshire and we would spend the rest of the summer there, before once again hitting the road. Dave would relate everything he had witnessed and partook of in Woodstock. The "Baby Boomers" are from that time period. We would go to Chicago and the start of our beloved Route 66 and once again set our sights on traveling it from start to finish.

Chapter 10

"On the Road Again"

I kinda feel sorry for the person who doesn't like to travel. There is so much to see in this beautiful country. I guess it was for this reason, after I left the workforce, I took a job where I got to travel the whole US. Even today, those places Dave and I visited back then draw the same "WOW" as they did seeing them in person for the first time, even if it was through a drug induced haze.

Did you know there is a "Petrified Forest" in Arizona?

Here's one you never would have guessed. Southern California is the largest producer of "cotton" in the United States! I've stood in those cotton fields, reached down and picked raw cotton off the stem!

I used to have a couple of rocks I picked up from the bottom of Mount Rushmore. Not ones bought in a nick-knack store, but ones I picked up off the ground at the foot of the mountain.

Hike down through the Grand Canyon, build a small camp fire, smoke a joint then go catch your meal out of the Colorado River! Beautiful and tasty.

The red's bouncing of the canyon walls at sunset are stunning when witnessed firsthand.

There is so much you can do and see when you have no time table to go by, or all the rules and regulations that you need to follow in our time today. Back in the late 60's early 70's the world was a different place. Our country was a different country. Most had respect for the other.

If you were "stupid" you didn't need someone doing all sorts of tests on you, or trying to figure out which parent's gene caused the stupidity! No, you accepted the fact you were "stupid" and was proud of it! Outside of our experience in Texas, Dave and I never once feared for our lives while on the road. I don't recall the last time I saw a person hitching. Do you? And if you did, would you stop and give him a ride? Probably not.

Back then our jails were filled with, not murderers, but some petty criminals. This acted as a deterrent to others. Today, nothing is done to those who riot, destroy other people's property and nothing is done to them to deter future bad behavior. A slap on the ass or a boot in the butt, or even Sister Mary's ruler across the knuckles that was all the deterrent I needed back then.

WOW! Did I get off the subject? Sorry.

Getting out of Chicago was harder than getting in. It became apparent the only way we were getting out of the city was to walk or take a bus. So, to the bus station and two tickets to Springfield which was, for me, the beginning of Route 66. But we did travel it from its origin and would travel it to its end. You couldn't be in Springfield without visiting all the Abe Lincoln sites and history there. Hitching out of Springfield was a lot easier than Chicago and within no time we were truly on the road again, sitting in the back of a pickup drinking a beer which the two shared with us and in return we were sharing a joint.

Being a huge Elvis fan we decided to leave Route 66 and venture to Memphis. With our cardboard signs reading Memphis, everyone who gave us a lift had their own Elvis stories. Even one guy who had went target shooting with him in his back yard. WOW! I wanted whatever he was smoking. He dumped us out somewhere in the middle of nowhere which proved to be an interesting time.

Being next to a river, we decided to take a swim. At rivers edge, we discovered we weren't alone. About a hundred feet from where we stood was a pool and in it were five girls, and spying the pile of clothes on a rock, told Dave and myself they were skinny dipping. When we noticed them, they also noticed us. All five gave us a welcoming wave to join them which we did. On the bank of the river, Dave and I shed our cloths, rolled and lit a couple of joints, then ventured into the pool of freezing water to join them. It wasn't long before I lost the shyness I have had all through school and at the start of this trip. All I'll write here is if you ever get a chance to be with five naked girls and a few joints of good pot! Well!

I don't recall any of their names, but two would join Dave and I to Memphis, then to San Antonio, Texas where we would part ways.

I guess I will name the two girls Debbie and Janis seeing I can't recall their real names. Deb, I recall was a full figured girl and Janis couldn't have weighed more than ninety pounds. They both said they were nineteen and from Wisconsin if I remember correctly, and were hitching to Dallas where Deb had a brother she hadn't seen in a long time, who was getting married.

She came from a poor family and didn't have money for bus fare to Dallas, so she got a girlfriend to hitch with her. She told us that she and her brother used to hitch a lot back home even when they were young teenagers. Janis was Deb's girlfriend. I use that word correctly which we would learn later. Turns out, Dave and I were the first guys she had ever been with. I can recall as though it was yesterday, sitting around the campfire under a blanket of stars watching those two perform their dance of love and eventually we would be waved over, an invitation to join them. After Memphis and seeing Graceland, it was on to Texas.

Hitching with two girls wearing short shorts and halter tops or just a colorful frilly bra proved to be interesting. Sometimes the two would see a car coming and as it approached, wrap their arms around each other and kiss. What looks that would get from the passing motorist. We swam naked in many a stream or river from

Memphis to Dallas. Sometimes the two would go off by themselves for some together time alone. At this time, Dave was into uppers and downers and smoking lots of weed. Me? I had discovered the world of LSD, although I had experienced it on several different occasions, it now became my drug of choice. That was in a nutshell, our trip to Dallas.

Once there, Deb called her brother who came out to meet us and welcomed us into his home. After showers, he brought us all to visit Daley Plaza, where on November 22, 1963, President John F. Kennedy was assassinated. Dave and I refused the offer to stay the night, although seeing how friendly brother, sister, Janis, and fiancée had become, it probably would have been a memorable one. Instead, we had him give us a ride way out of the city and put us on the road to San Antonio and the Alamo.

Chapter 11

"Hippie Hill Park, Austin, TX."

Our first ride was with a cowboy wearing a large hat, and blasting some old Beatles tune from his radio which had cracked speakers which were mounted in a couple of homemade plywood boxes which took up half of the rear seat. After listening to "I Want To Hold Your Hand" for the one-hundredth time at volume ten through cracked speakers, you draw a disliking for the Beatles. Although I never liked them before now either.

As it turned out, this ride was going to Austin which is where there was a large Hippie gathering place called Hippie Hollow Park located around Lake Travis. This being where we were headed the year before when we ended up in Amarillo instead, which nearly cost us our lives. The name Hippie Hollow Park was giving to the McGregor County Park shortly after Woodstock and the influx of Hippie's to that region.

Our first day there was a hot one and true to what we had heard many were nude even though there were signs forbidding nudity. Because this was a central gathering spot for the Hippie Culture and as long as they created no trouble they were pretty much left alone.

Dave and I spent probably a week there. Most of the time in the nude along with others, and sleeping out under the stars and eating whatever some of the girls would bring around. Once a day, a station wagon would appear and two old ladies would get out, open the back and remove two large boxes which held all sorts of food and soda's. Looking back now, I wonder how many lives they influenced later on in life.

Here it is, forty-six years later and I still recall those two. No fanfare, no hello's or waves, just humbly taking those two boxes from the back of the wagon and sitting them on the ground and driving off. I could picture my mom and Aunt Rose being those two.

Hippie Hollow is also where we would experience a new drug. Peyote. Having used Peyote, it's easy to see why Santa Anna took over 1,500 soldiers over 10 days to defeat only about 250 in the Alamo. They were probably all messed up on Peyote. There are lots of ways to take this foul, bitter, tasting drug which is derived from a specific cactus found in Texas and Mexico.

Peyote was a form of hallucinogenic. The main substance that makes up peyote is mescaline. If you smoked pot, you probably have done mescaline. Lots of times the peyote buttons which contain the mescaline was ground up into powder and sprinkled over the pot leaves and was smoked.

As I said, although it gave a feeling of body separating from your soul and you could have a deep spiritual experience, the taste was horrible and it usually made you nauseous.

It was here where I learned how to do peyote and not have a nauseous feeling or the horrible taste in your mouth. You're waiting for this, right? You took the peyote button and shoved it up your butt. That's right. Up the butt. Your body would still absorb the mescaline without going past your taste buds or ending in your stomach. So the phrase, "I'm tripping my ass off," came from this.

Although nudity was tolerated, public lovemaking was not. Everyone sort of policed each other as far as this was concerned. As a matter of fact, you were expected to interrupt anyone who was so engaged. Of course, under the cover of darkness was a different story. The darkness might make it impossible to see, but it did nothing to your hearing! Our time spent here was ones of absolute freedom. Smoking weed, laying nude in the hot Texas sun, more eye candy than one could handle, but, soon it was time to leave.

The rides to San Antonio were non exciting. For the most part, Texas was just a flat, hot piece of land we had to past through. If needed, we would return and hang out around here for the winter months. No way were we going to be anywhere north.

Our ride dropped us off just before we got to San Antonio with a suggestion to hide our backpacks and not to spend a lot of time wondering around. Here Hippie's and long hair's weren't really welcome. We hid our backpacks and entered the city and visited the Alamo. I have visited the Alamo several times over the years and it still amazes me how small it is.

From here we hitched northwest to El Paso, then onto Las Cruces and Albuquerque where we would once again pick up our beloved Route 66.

Chapter 12

"California Dreaming"

It felt good to be back on Route 66 and heading west to California. There was one place I wanted to go to and it was in the very northeastern tip of Arizona. This place was called the Four State Monument. It is the only place in the states where four states come together at perfect ninety degree angles. There is a plaque there where you can put a hands in two states and your feet in two states placing you in all four states at the same time. Utah, Colorado, New Mexico and Arizona. After this, it was back onto Route 66 and onto Santa Monica, California where Dave and I walked into the Pacific Ocean, completing our cross country jaunt.

From there, we went to Hollywood to walk the Sidewalk of the Stars. If you think California has some weird people today, you needed to be there in '69. From some street people we learned of a place where we could crash for the night. It was in an old abandoned warehouse where someone had set up some cots and invited homeless and wonderers, such as ourselves, a place to crash. There were a couple of Hippie girls wondering around being very friendly if you had some weed or other drugs. As always, Dave had some pot so one of the girls spent some time with us both. Two days later we found we both had the crabs! Going into a drug store we picked up some crab shampoo and went into a thrift store and found some clothes. After a good shower we through away those clothes and put on our new ones. Looking back now, I'm surprised we never caught worse than crabs.

We hitched up the coast and spent several days walking the shore line and sleeping on the small, tucked away beaches. Somewhere around Monterey, we talked about what to do. I wanted to go back and travel around the southwest and Dave wanted to go back up to San Francisco, so we separated.

I headed for Fresno where I figured it would be easier hitching than staying on the coastal highway. Plans were to just meet again in the spring at my house in New Hampshire. He could call my mom and she would know when I planned to be back.

I spent that winter in southern Arizona, New Mexico, and Texas. I slept out under the stars, while once again pumping gas and washing windows. Then visiting all those places, I read about in westerns and saw on TV, as a kid sitting in front of our black & white TV drinking a cup of hot cocoa and eating one of mom's homemade donuts covered with powdered sugar. The show Tombstone being the one I liked more than most.

Being in Arizona, I went to Yuma then to Casa Grande, down to Tucson and ending up in Tombstone. The only building from the original town was the Birdcage which was a saloon, brothel, gambling hall and a theater. If you don't know much about Tombstone, except for the gunfight at the OK Corral, do a web search. Did you know that Tombstone had a bowling alley, ice cream parlor, and one-hundred ten saloons?

I had given up my Hippie clothes and settled for some jean bell bottoms, instead of the brightly colored printed ones, a plain tee shirt and jean jacket. Gone was the flowered shirts and headband. I kept the hair though but shaved off the beard. I met a lot of people in Tombstone, as it is now a tourist attraction and I would be there for almost a month. I recall one night sleeping out under a blanket of stars on a brightly lit night from the largest silver moon I have ever seen.

After having done some LSD, I was awakened by something wet on my face. Opening my eyes, I found myself looking eye to eye with a big, black buffalo. Needless to say, I was outta there in a shot. Never once looking back to see if he was chasing me or not. Jumping over a barbed wired fence I stopped running. My heart pounding in my chest caused a steady, ka-thump, ka-thump, ka-thump sound to my ears. Sitting down, I must have fallen asleep. When I woke up with the warm morning sun on my face, to my surprise, I was back in my little camp. I sat up shaking my head and wondering how the heck did I get back here and where the heck is that buffalo?

Chapter 13

"Mardi Gras"

Every state has that one city and event for which it is known by. For Louisiana, the city is New Orleans and the event is Mardi Gras.

Mardi Gras is held in many countries and even other states and cities in the US, it's just the New Orleans Mardi Gras is the most famous and talked about. After getting the exact date Mardi Gras would take place, I headed there with plenty of time for travel. Mardi Gras was everything I had heard it would be and then some. One never lacked for drink or joint.

Back then, the police weren't as strict as you hear about today. Basically, the only thing asked was if you wore a costume with a mask was that you removed it when entering any kind of business.

The showing of breasts for beads has been around for a long time and I sure got my eyes full. I would look for girls wearing lots of beads and they were the ones to watch. It wasn't only the young girls either! No sir! There were moms and grannies more than willing to bear breast for beads. I would take up and stay with a couple of these more mature ladies. I won't go into all the hot details, but I will say with these two that it was a nonstop adventure of share and share alike.

Crazy, crazy, place it was. The party never ended.

After New Orleans, I headed for the Gulf Shore of Florida for the remainder of the winter, spending time in the Florida Panhandle. Did you know that the Florida Panhandle has some of the largest cattle ranches in the States? Florida was an easy state to hitch in. Just about every ride I got, I was offered a place to spend the night. I was born in Florida in a little town known as Polk City, which is located between Lakeland and Orlando. There hadn't been an address on my birth certificate so I never found the place where I was born. I knew it wasn't in a hospital because I was delivered by a mid-wife. It was now early spring in New Hampshire and time to phone home and let them all know I was on the way home.

Chapter 14

"Tubing"

One of the more fun ways we traveled was by inner-tube. I doubt today any kid would know what an inner tube is.

We had been hitching for some time when we were picked up by a VW Bus, loaded with pot smoking Hippies who were on the way to some river to swim, tube, get stoned, and drink beer. "Yahoo," our kind of people. By the time we arrived at the river, Dave and I were well on the way of being "wrecked" another name for being stoned or high. I recall it to be a very wide river which flowed into this large pool the size of maybe two football fields. Looking back now, I see we were on a little river which flowed into the larger Mississippi River.

As beer coolers were unloaded and inner tubes blown up, I wondered why there were no girls around. I didn't have to wonder for very long. About the time the inner tubes were blown up, a station wagon arrived and several girls, whooping and hollering got out followed by this cloud of smoke. (I would be reminded of this moment years later while watching the movie "Up In Smoke" when Cheech and Chong exited their vehicle in that movie amongst a cloud of pot smoke.) We learned that these girls belonged to no one. They were all friends who hung out together and partied. Dave and I fit right in as far as everyone was concerned. They all had beer and pot, we had some pot and LSD.

Halter tops and short shorts were their outfit that day. I half expected them all to shed their clothes. When we guys ended up doing so, only two of the girls did, and throughout the day they exhibited and extended to all us guys the meaning of "Free Love" for which the decade was noted for. Tripping on LSD with your naked butt in the water and having a naked girl bouncing around on you was quiet the experience and one could tell it wasn't a first time for either girl. It became apparent they were invited for this very reason and they didn't mind including Dave and I in on the good times. Sorta like a water bed but wet.

One of the tubes had a piece of plywood over it to hold the coolers and pot. The other tubes, you just planted your naked butt into the hole and floated around, feet and hands dangling in the cool water. The games of love that could be played out on one of these tubes was interesting to watch, or better yet, take part in!!!

When it was time to leave, Dave asked them if we could have a couple of their tubes and we were given a couple. Later on, tubing from time to time became our way of travel. We found that tubes could be purchased for little to nothing at gas station that changed tires. They always had some patched tubes laying around for poor travelers with flats as well as the kids wanting them just for tubing. Most of the time we got them free for pumping gas for a couple of hours.

We actually constructed our own Huck Finn type of raft using several inner tubes tied together along with odd pieces of boards and old sign parts laid across them for decking. We would spend about three weeks on this section of the Mississippi River having acquired several more tubes and tying them together along with more pieces of wood collected from old abandoned docks and homes, and old barns. We had ourselves quiet the raft. We made a lean to type tent from an old piece of tarp to protect us from the sun during the day and the rain.

Anytime we saw an abandoned building or shack we would stop to investigate and see what we could find that might be of some use. We had quite the collection of cookware, dishes, silverware, books, and toys! All courtesy from the many abandoned buildings we went through.

Today, as I drive the US, I can't pass by an old abandoned house, barn, factory, gas station, hotel, etc. without stopping to investigate. Reliving a time long passed. I have thousands of digital photographs of these abandoned buildings, barns, outdoor movie theaters, etc. I found an old fishing pole once, so we dug up some worms and that night we enjoyed some fresh fish which we cooked over an open fire, right there on the deck of our raft. Somewhere we had picked up a piece of tin roofing and formed it into a shape we could build a fire in. Catfish anyone?

Looking back, I wonder if anyone saw the eerie glow of a fire floating down the Mississippi in the darkness of the night and wondered just what the heck they were seeing. Real life Tom Sawyer and Huck Finn we were! From time to time, someone in a boat or canoe would paddle out to say hello to the two strange looking guys on a funny looking raft. We had picked up a couple paddles to help steer the raft, when we needed to.

You might have seen pictures of the Mississippi River but they don't compare with seeing it from a makeshift inner tube raft. Just an AWESOME sight. Floating on the river in the sunsets and sunrises, absolutely stunning.

Two things we learned the first time we did this was, you needed some kind of bug spray and a mosquito netted hat. We would purchase a couple bee keeper's bonnets which worked great along with some tent netting we purchased at an Army and Navy store. The bugs were endless. Anytime throughout our travels that we wanted to just lay back and take it easy, if there was a river, we would get ourselves a couple inner tubes and just float a while.

We talked about tubing the length of the Mississippi some day in the future, along with the Colorado River, but we never did. I don't recall now why we didn't, other than when we returned home, life caught up with us and we went our separate ways. Plus, it was now the beginning of the 70's and times were a changing.

When the 60's were over, it was over.

CHAPTER 15

"Life Under the Overpass"

You have probably seen them on TV or maybe in person even, the bums and homeless people who make their homes living under overpasses. I know you have all seen a motorcycle pulled under one during that downpour of rain. Anyway, if you look up at the very end of the overpass where it meets the ground, there is a ledge. It is about four feet wide which passing motorists don't even see when speeding by, which also means they don't see you. So it becomes a perfect place to call home from time to time. Many a night was spent sleeping on that four feet of concrete, especially when it rained if there weren't any barns or abandoned buildings around. It also offered a cooler place to rest on those vary hot days when rides were scarce.

Dave carried the darn dish stuff in his backpack. One of these items being a little folding metal stove which used for Sterno fuel which came in a can that fit into the folding stove. It gave off a lot of heat where you could boil water, heat up canned food, or use it for heat. It was funny to watch as a car would stop under it and someone would hop out to take a leak, and half way through it, you yelled down at him and watch him jump, peeing all over themselves. Sometimes you had to share this space with mourning doves, pigeons, and other hitch hikers such as Billy and Sue.

This overpass was right at the exit our ride was getting off at, so we had him drop us off at the overpass, since it had just started to rain. As we started up the steep incline, we heard voices calling from across the highway. On the other side were two people who waved us over and clearly to see were Hippies like us. Their names were Billy and Sue. I remember this because a couple of years earlier B J Thomas had come out with a song by the same name. Unlike us, they lived nearby and were hitching into the city to meet up with friends. Turns out, Billy and Sue were brother and sister. The four of us climbed the steep bank and sat on the concrete ledge sharing some stories. Billy said he was twenty and Sue was eighteen, although she appeared younger and sat quietly just staring straight ahead, watching cars as they passed by. Soon, the question was asked if we had any drugs. We told him we had some pot and some LSD. At the mention of LSD, Billy's eyes seemed to jump in their sockets.

Well! To make a long story short, we ended up trading Billy two rolled joints and two hits of LSD for some playtime with his sister, Sue. If I recall correctly, he got the better half of the deal!!!

The other use of an overpass was when we would get stopped by a local cop or even a Highway Patrol Officer and was told we couldn't hitch hike in city limits or their jurisdiction. When we asked how far out of town was that, they answered, "When you couldn't see any buildings." Well, we looked for an overpass to stand under, look around, and seeing no buildings, continued hitching.

CHAPTER 16

"Homeward Bound"

"Hello. Will you accept the collect charges?"

With that sentence, I was headed home. My time on the road would come to an end shortly. Right around seventeen-hundred miles, I figured, was how many miles it was to home.

I relentlessly held up my sign for the passing motorist getting on interstate 95. Most of the vehicles had northern plates and I figured they were the snow bunnies headed home themselves after wintering in Florida. The license plate was from Maine and attached to a small RV driven by an old man wearing a colorful Hawaiian shirt and shorts smoking a fat cigar.

I'll remember always the smell of that cigar and wondered why the woman sitting next to him wearing a muscle beach style shirt, obviously braless, and shorts, put up with the smell. Then I noticed it. Between her lips was the fattest joint I had ever seen. It must have been rolled with five or six Zig Zag rolling papers. As I got in she took my back pack and tossed it into the back, smiled, and handed me the joint. I was going to turn it down, but decided to go with it and see what was going to happen. They were indeed from Maine and headed home after wintering in Florida, and yes, they would be passing through New Hampshire and would drop me off at my door.

I couldn't believe my good fortune. They had been married for forty-five years, having been marred in their teens and now lived in an open relationship. He could no longer perform and she was like she had been at twenty. They kept their marriage together by him agreeing to let her take on lovers, but he had to be present.

It wasn't long before that RV was parked in a rest area with the imaginary sign hung on the door which read, "IF THIS VEHICLE IS A ROCKING, DON'T COME KNOCKING." The drive to New Hampshire was one of a hundred stops at rest areas! Enough said.

True to their word, they brought me right to my house where Dave was already. After my hello's with the folks, we left and went down on the boardwalk. As we walked around I pulled Dave aside and quickly filled him in on this couple. They both really hit it off with Dave, and when they left, he went with them onto Maine.

That was the last time I saw Dave. Over the years I would hear something about him and try to locate him, but never did. Through my reaching out through social media I have learned of his passing and parts of his life, which I will keep private.

Later in life as told before, I traveled the US with my job, and would cross over the old Route 66 many times.

It is now Interstate 40, but gives reference to Historic Route 66 along the way.

Passing some of the old abandoned and run down gas stations along the route, I have often wondered if just maybe that was one of the gas stations I had pumped gas at, forty some odd years ago. The same with old deserted factories with all their windows broken out, once alive with the sounds of machines running.

And stopping to get gas, is that older lady behind the register the same beauty that flashed me when washing her windshield or one I skinny dipped with in the river? Smoked a joint with under a blanket of silver twinkling stars? Who knows? Maybe.

I hope all of you who are reading this got a small window of what it was like to have lived back in the 60's and how others did also. The only time we feared for our lives was in Texas. Today, you fear for your life walking out your front door, which by the way, was never locked back then.

Your kids will never know the joy of finding and turning in those couple of coke bottles at the little store on the corner of your street for a handful of hard candy. At my age now, I might not be able to tell you what I did yesterday, but I can sing word for word, "California Dreamin'", "Hotel California", "Purple Haze" and "Hey Joe."

Psychedelic music, pot, LSD, long hair, colorful clothes, rock and roll, riding a bike without a helmet, and rock festivals such as Woodstock. These are just a few of those things we enjoyed or experienced that helped shape the 60's.

OH! And let's not ever forget Sister Mary's ruler!!!

The End

Epilogue

Returning home, I continued for a while to live as I had been. My favorite drug, LSD was still very popular so I started dealing in it, making thousands of dollars, but as my 'old man' once told me, "Son. A fool and his money will soon part ways." Proved to be correct.

I had bought all the things that I thought would make me happy, but they did not. Looking around me, I realized I was missing one thing. The companionship of a loving woman. She would come in a surprise and at a time I was hitting the bottom of the barrel, sort of speaking.

MJ worked at Dunkin' Donuts, a place I visited quite often, when dealing. I guess if there is such a thing as love at first sight, well, she was it to me. But she was a Mormon girl and for sure these two worlds didn't go together. So, if I was to get anywhere with MJ I needed to change, and that is what I did. Through her, I met two Mormon Missionary Sisters, got my hair cut, dropped the drugs, and was baptized into the Mormon religion and started a relationship with MJ. I couldn't be happier.

Putting away old ways, gaining brand new friends, and generally being loved by her family, MJ and I started to live out an existence both of us thought would lead to marriage. But old ways slowly crept back into my life. Desires I thought I had shelved returned and took over.

When an old girlfriend came back into my life, MJ and I parted. I would go on to marry the old girlfriend and have three sons, before our marriage would end. I would marry the woman who finished forming me into the person I've become over the years, and who I am still married to today.

You've been asked, I'm sure. If you could go back in time, what would you change or like to do over if anything? There is an old country western song by Chris Ledoux that goes something like this: "Out of all the things I've done, there's really only one I'd like to change, out here, between the rainbows and the rain." For me, that would be MJ. I would like to see where that road might of lead, but you can't, so you live life the way it's been dealt out to you.

Today at sixty-six and married for thirty-two years, I must say I've lived a full life. As my health fades, I blame it all on the year 1969! That's my story and I'm sticking to it!!! I have had three heart operations where they inserted three stents, two strokes, where I have had to overcome left side paralysis, four bouts with pneumonia, and going on seven years now with Parkinson's disease.

As stated, I have a loving wife of thirty-two years. I have three sons, two step-children, nine grand-kids. I have built a successful career in the Spa Industry, building manufacturing plants in Connecticut, Illinois, and Indiana. I have traveled to forty-eight of our fifty states, and lots of Canadian travel as well as the Caribbean Islands and a couple of Mexico's vacation spots.

I have written and published five western novels in both English and Spanish, and this little book titled, "Between the White Line and the Fence Post" I have written and have had recorded in Nashville three songs.

Every decade is defined by different events that sets them off from each other, and no decade was more defined then the 60's. I wish that Dave and I could have stayed in touch. I wonder if he ever shared these events with family and friends as I have. I wonder if he ever thought of these days and wondered what I was up to, or just sat with a grin on his face, shaking his head remembering some instance which we had lived out and survived.

I have found that one must be able to change with the times. As much as the 60's had an effect on my life, when it was over, it was over, and I was needing to change. Every day in life, you make choices. Those choices have lasting effects on family, friends, work, and you personally. A lot of my friends didn't survive the 60's. Health, drugs, and war took them away.

Sometimes I think they were the lucky ones, but then I look around at my life, and family and what I've accomplished and shake my head no, I'm the lucky one. Although it has been a tough battle and the world today is filled with so much hate, it seems like there isn't a

country that isn't at war with another. These are times
where I think we, as a people, need to stop, grow some
hair, put on some colorful cloths, light a big bonfire, chill
out and pass around the bong pipe, joints, micro-dot acid
and cold beer. Then dig out the old vinyl, sit back and
listen to some psychedelic music along with a little Ravi.
I'm one of the lucky ones. I lived the 60's, took
everything that it had to give and more, and I'm still here.
I've been asked a hundred times, knowing what I know
now, would I do it again. My answer is always the same.
YES.

For my life as I know it today, I owe to my loving
wife who stood beside me through the hard times of
change. Through the up-rooting our home and moving as
I built a career. Through the "Flash-backs" which at
times seemed so real. Without the love and support of my
loving wife, I don't think I would have been able to
survive those times when the past demanded my
attention.

But she was there. And here I am. A walking, talking,
breathing, human being. A survivor of the greatest era in
the history of the world.

E.C. HERBERT